The Five Mile Press

The Five Mile Press Pty Ltd
22 Summit Road Noble Park
Victoria 3174 Australia
Phone: +61 3 9790 5000
Fax: +61 3 9790 6888
Email: publishing@fivemile.com.au

This format first published 2002
5 4 3 2

Printed in Singapore

National Library of Australia
Cataloguing-in-Publication data
Barber, Shirley
Shirley Barber's let's look at colours.

ISBN 1 86503 626 9

1. Colours - Juvenile literature.
I. Title. II. Title: Let's look at colours.

Shirley Barber's
Let's Look at
Colours

At the back of this book, there is a special colour palette
showing the names of the colours featured in the illustrations.

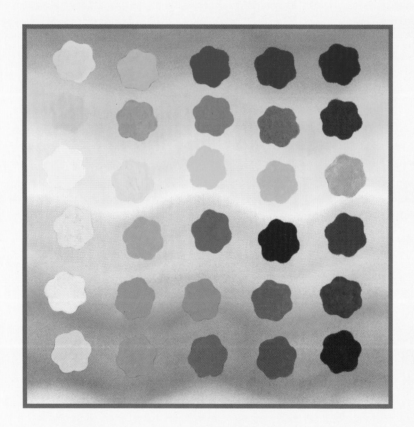

Children can use this palette to help them identify the
many different shades of colour in each picture.

Shirley Barber's

Let's Look at Colours

The Five Mile Press

These little workmice are painting
the toy fire engine red.
What a mess they are making!

Let's look at the colours!
How many different shades of red
can you see?

The orange leaves are falling from
the trees and the frisky cats are playing with them.

Let's look at the colours!
How many different shades of orange
can you see?

Teddy and his sister Tiffany are playing among the yellow buttercups. Lots of butterflies are coming to say "Hello!"

How many different shades of yellow can you see?

Famous Professor Spot O'Doggarty has been searching for the rare green smiling Jungle Frog — and he's found it!

How many different shades of green can you see?

Princess Mewlinda
has gone to bed early to read her book.
You can tell that her favourite colour is blue!

How many different shades of blue
can you see?

Queen Kitty loves gardening.
She is growing beautiful purple pansies
on the castle terrace.

How many different shades of purple
can you see?

These naughty kittens have pulled out some balls of wool. The little pup is playing with the blue wool.

Let's look at all the coloured wool. How many different colours can you see?

Pale Pink

Rose Pink

Primary Red

Poster Red

Crimson

Pale Orange

Orange

Vermilion

Burnt Orange

Sienna

Pale Yellow

Primrose

Primary Yellow

Cadmium Yellow

Yellow Ochre

Pale Green

Leaf Green

Viridian

Bottle Green

Olive Green

Pale Blue

Turquoise Blue

Sky Blue

Primary Blue

Ultramarine

Mauve

Light Violet

Dark Violet

Magenta

Imperial Purple